Original title:
Buds of Brilliance

Copyright © 2025 Creative Arts Management OÜ
All rights reserved.

Author: Colin Harrington
ISBN HARDBACK: 978-1-80566-660-8
ISBN PAPERBACK: 978-1-80566-945-6

## A Glance at Tomorrow

In the garden of dreams, seeds of laughter grow,
With a sprinkle of giggles, they put on a show.
Dancing in sunlight, they wiggle and spin,
Whispering secrets of the fun we're in.

With helmets made of petals, they zip through the air,
Chasing after butterflies, without a care.
Each bloom a comedian, with jokes to retell,
Filling the meadow with a chuckle and yell.

Worms wear tiny glasses, critters join in,
Squirrels swap stories while pulling a grin.
Even the daisies don silly hats,
As they plan a parade for the old garden rats.

Life's a circus of colors, quite the favorite show,
With each twirl and tumble, there's always a glow.
So let's tiptoe through laughter, like soft morning dew,
Tomorrow's a canvas; let's paint it anew!

## Nature's Quiet Revelations

In the garden, whispers play,
Flowers joke in their own way.
A daisy giggles at the sun,
While tulips nudge, 'Come, let's run!'

Butterflies sport their silly dance,
Bees are buzzing, taking a chance.
'Pollinate!' they bumble with glee,
But watch your snacks, don't eat the bee!

## Threads of Enlightenment

A spider spins in spiraled jest,
Weaving lines, it thinks it's best.
A ladybug rolls her eyes with flair,
'That's too much work, is life so rare?'

In these threads, humor does thrive,
In the garden, all come alive.
Laughter blooms on every vine,
As nature plots its quirky line.

## **Awakening Harmony**

The sun peeks in, a cheeky grin,
Waking crickets, let's begin!
They chirp jokes that don't quite rhyme,
But laughter flows, oh so sublime!

The brook babbles with such delight,
Tickling stones all through the night.
'Hey, watch it!' giggles every fish,
As they swim past, granting a wish.

## The Promise of Spring

Spring arrives with a flourish,
Telling winter, 'You must nourish.'
Chirping birds plan their next show,
'Who's got the best and brightest glow?'

A rabbit hops, in dapper style,
Grooming flowers with a smile.
'Hey, look at me!' they chirp in sync,
As colors bloom in winks and pink!

**Nature's Gentle Battleground**

In the garden, ants parade,
Marching like tiny solders,
Each leaf a battlefield,
Though they wield no boulders.

The daisies laugh and sway,
While the clovers play it cool,
A tug-of-war with sunshine,
Nature's own crazy school.

## Rays of Opportunity

The sun's a cheeky jester,
Playing hide and seek,
It tickles the morning dew,
Making flowers giggle and peek.

Bumblebees buzz with glee,
On petals soft and round,
Sipping nectar, having fun,
In their little playground.

## Outpour of Vibrance

Colors splash like paintball fights,
Rainbows on display,
Petunias blush in purple hues,
As sunbeams bounce and play.

Silly squirrels throw a party,
With acorns on the floor,
Nature dances wildly,
As critters shout, "Encore!"

## The Heart of a Flower

A sunflower grins wide and bright,
In shades of gold and green,
It winks at the passing bees,
"Come, join my funky scene!"

Petals twirl like ballerinas,
In the warm, soft breeze,
Each bloom a little mischief,
Whispering secrets with ease.

## Seeds of Inspiration

In the garden of quirky dreams,
Seeds sprout, bursting at the seams.
Some sprout legs, others wear hats,
Dancing around like silly cats.

Ideas pop, just like corn,
From each tiny plant, new thoughts are born.
They giggle and wiggle in sunlight's embrace,
Turning the garden into a wild chase.

## Nature's Hidden Gleam

Beneath the soil, secrets hide,
Giggling worms play peekaboo side.
They whisper jokes to worms aloof,
While dreaming of the world's great roof.

Sprouts poke up with a cheeky grin,
Waving at bees as they buzz and spin.
"Catch me if you can!" they tease and gleam,
Nature's got jokes, or so it seems!

## Luminous Growth

Tiny tendrils stretch and play,
Reaching for the sun's warm ray.
With each inch, a chuckle shared,
As petals prance, they're well-prepared.

A sunflower winks, "Look at me!"
While daisies laugh in wild glee.
They're growing tall, just for the fun,
To tickle the clouds before they run.

## Awakening Splendor

In the morning dew, a surprise,
Colors burst like painted skies.
Each blossom grins, a vibrant face,
As if they've just won a funny race.

Petals flutter, gossip spreads,
"Who wore it best?" the wind in treads.
As laughter fills the blooming air,
Nature's jesters, beyond compare.

**In the Embrace of Nature**

In a world of playful glee,
Squirrels dance on a tall tree.
They toss acorns like a ball,
Nature's joke, we share it all.

Pigeons wear their hats askew,
Mice play poker, how 'bout you?
The sun winks with a golden grin,
While flowers giggle, let's begin!

**Portraits of Change**

A worm in shades of bright neon,
Plans a party, come and be drawn.
The petals shout with colors new,
While clouds debate their favorite hue.

Cats in sunglasses strut in style,
While dogs dig holes, but not for a smile.
Change is chaos with a twist,
Laughter's pretty hard to resist!

## Kaleidoscope of Hopes

A butterfly with polka dots,
Swaps her shoes with big toe knots.
Hopes like bubbles float and sway,
Popping laughter on the way.

Silly dreams in colors bright,
Turning wrongs into pure delight.
Every giggle plants a seed,
In this world of joyful greed.

## **Enchanted Growth**

In the garden of silly charms,
Teddy bears with dance moves and arms.
A sunflower does the cha-cha slide,
While cacti cheer, all filled with pride.

Lettuce rolls down the grassy hill,
Tomatoes juggle for the thrill.
Magic sprouts in laughter's glow,
As we watch this wild show grow!

**Embracing the Early Light**

Morning giggles stretch and yawn,
The rooster's crow feels like a song.
Waking flowers shake their heads,
Saying, "Sleep in? No way! Get up instead!"

Sunshine tickles petals bright,
Even bees are taking flight.
Dancing shadows on the ground,
All around, joy is found.

## Echoes of New Beginnings

A sprout peeks with a hopeful grin,
"I swear I'm growing faster than kin!"
Worms below roll their eyes,
"Tea parties here, much to our surprise!"

Ants march in with tiny flags,
Planning picnics, no time for drags.
Grasshoppers strum on a leafy lute,
While ladybugs dance in their shiny suit.

**Unseen Beauty in the Cracks**

Through concrete sidewalks flowers bloom,
"Finding light? A splendid gloom!"
Cracks in the pavement, art on display,
"Perfect for selfies, hey! Hooray!"

Weeds host parties, loud and proud,
"No lawnmower's gonna silence our crowd!"
Nature laughs at rules we make,
Jokes in bloom, oh for goodness' sake!

## Budding Dreams Beneath the Surface

Beneath the soil, secrets lie,
Little roots whisper, "Let's try!"
Mice ponder, "What's the big deal?"
Dreams of growth with every meal!

Daisies plot their great escape,
"We'll break free and become drapes!"
They giggle softly, then take flight,
Chasing sunbeams, oh what a sight!

## **Blossoming Spirits**

In the garden of laughs, we play,
Tiny hopes dance in a silly ballet.
With petals of dreams, we twirl and spin,
Laughter erupts as we dive right in.

A daisy in pajamas, what a sight,
Jokes bloom brightly, taking flight.
Silly sunflowers, with faces so wide,
Tickle our senses, a joy to abide.

Jellybeans sprouting, oh what a treat,
Marshmallow clouds beneath our feet.
We frolic with whimsy, our giggles loud,
These frothy emotions make us proud.

So let's sip on sunshine and swing from the vine,
Our spirits bring color, and how they shine!
In this quirky garden, we'll find our cheer,
Embracing each moment, holding them dear.

## Flickers of Magic

In a realm where quirks like to play,
Silly wands flash bright, in a goofy way.
A rabbit in glasses, quite the charmer,
Calls forth laughter, oh what a bomber!

With broomsticks that wiggle, and brooms that giggle,
Everyone's dancing, it's quite the wiggle.
Fairies with pizza, what a grand feast,
Serving up joy, we're never the least.

Confetti sprinkles from magical spouts,
Creating tall castles made of our shouts.
Sneaky gnomes with their tickling schemes,
Sprout silly pranks, and jubilant dreams.

So let's ride on the waves of this cheer,
With wonder each day that brings us near.
In this dance of laughter and glee,
Flickers of magic, for you and me!

## **Vibrant Emergence**

In colorful chaos, we burst into bloom,
Giggles and wiggles fill every room.
Like balloons gone wild, we float in the air,
Coloring moments with laughter to share.

Rainbow confetti, it sparkles and shines,
Grinning like kids who've outsmarted the shrines.
With daisies on cupcakes and sprinkles from joy,
All giggles and grins from each girl and boy.

Twinkling fireflies, with bright little quirks,
Dance through the night as our laughter works.
In this vibrant circus, we stand so tall,
Silliness reigns, in our grand carnival!

So come join our journey, it's an adventure indeed,
Where smiles grow wild, and silly hearts lead.
With every bright moment, let's shout, "Hooray!"
For tomorrow's giggles are just a play away!

## The Art of Becoming

With brushes of humor, we paint the sky,
Each stroke a chuckle, our laughter flies high.
Whimsical creatures tap dance through time,
In a world that's wobbly, oh so sublime.

Squiggles and giggles, a canvas of dreams,
Covering the chaos in candy-like themes.
A pickle in a tutu, quite the parade,
Reminds us to laugh while we orchestrate.

As cupcakes become kings, and jesters take flight,
Silly tales woven through day and night.
In this art of joy, let's swirl and blend,
Celebrating the giggles that never end.

So gather your palettes, let's color the day,
With petals of laughter to brighten our way.
In the masterpiece of life, let's take a stance,
For joy is the brush that creates our dance!

## The Dance of Transformation

Tiny seeds awake from dreams,
Wiggling like a worm in teams.
A flip, a flop, they jump and sing,
In garden tops, they pull off bling.

Sunshine tickles, laughter loud,
Petals strut, oh they are proud.
A circle here, a twisty throw,
Watch the leaves put on a show!

They twirl around in silly glee,
Twirling with the bumblebee.
A polka with a butterfly,
Bouncing high, they touch the sky.

In the soil, the roots all chatter,
"Look at us! We all are that-er!"
From fuzz to flair, they can't resist,
Plotting their blooms like a royal twist.

## The First Breath of Spring

Whispers hush through frozen air,
Nature giggles, shedding care.
The crocus peeks with tiny toes,
While frosty noses wiggle, who knows?

Silly dreams wake up the stones,
Feathered friends in funny phones.
They chirp and tweet, a morning song,
Telling winter, "You've been wrong!"

Sunshine's fingers, soft and warm,
Disturb the daisies' sleepy charm.
They stretch and yawn, "What a dream!
Dirt and dust? That's so extreme!"

Buzzy bees in fuzzy hats,
Dash like they're in silly spats.
Pollen party, don't you dare
Forget the flowers in your hair!

## Morning Dewdrops

Dewdrops dance on blades of grass,
Wearing glimmers as they pass.
Each droplet a tiny, wobbly fright,
Reflecting jokes in morning light.

They bounce and play, a liquid ball,
Tiptoeing on a leaf so small.
One slips off, it gives a shout,
"Did you see that? I'm gonna pout!"

A ladybug joins in the fun,
Rolling 'round until it's done.
"Make way for me!" it struts with pride,
Sliding sideways, it can't abide!

The sun peeks in with golden gleam,
While dewdrops make a silly team.
With giggles echoing in the air,
They splash and dash, without a care!

## Vibrant Echoes

Echoes of color bounce around,
In every nook, they swirl and sound.
Roses chuckle, lilies tease,
As daisies dance with utmost ease.

Colors laugh, they mix and blend,
Chasing each other, no need to mend.
Each shade whispers a silly tale,
Of winter's end and spring's great trail.

The tulips wear their fancy hats,
While sunflowers chat like giddy bats.
"I'm the tallest!" one flower shouts,
And all nearby break into routs!

Every petal, a comical sight,
Bouncing and twirling, what a delight!
In garden glee, they sing out loud,
For vibrant echoes, they are proud!

## New Horizons

Tiny sprouts in muddy shoes,
Dancing plants with silly views.
They giggle as they stretch and sway,
Thinking that they're here to play.

With sunlight snacks and rainfall cheer,
They chat about the clothes they wear.
One wears green, the other blue,
Wondering who looks best in dew!

They dream of stars and lands afar,
While aiming for the next candy bar.
With every wiggle, twist, and turn,
They plot a world where wonders burn.

Their roots are deep but heads are high,
Plotting mischief in the sky.
With every petal that bursts wide,
They're ready for a wild ride!

## The Radiant Cascade

A waterfall of colors bold,
With jolly hues that won't grow old.
Silly smirks on petals bright,
Bouncing in the warm sunlight.

They tumble down like laughing clowns,
Splashing puddles, flipping frowns.
Each drip is filled with laughter's song,
In this garden, nothing's wrong.

A yellow one says, "Take a leap!"
As pink responds, "Oh, let's not sleep!"
Together, they create a show,
Of giggles dancing, to and fro.

So here we bask in floral fun,
With vines that sway, and palmy sun.
In this cascade of laughter loud,
We find our joy among the crowd!

## **Petals and Possibilities**

Petals poke their heads up high,
Waving 'hello' to the sky.
With dreams of hosting flower fests,
They plan to show off their best vests.

One thinks he's a fashion star,
While another swears he'll go far.
"Look at my colors, bold and bright!"
"Mine glows in the moonlight!"

They bicker over who looks best,
While giggling at their flower quest.
"Let's bloom big and fill the air,
With laughter, joy, and flowers rare!"

With every breeze, they dance and sway,
Turning gardens into cabaret.
In a world of petals and cheer,
They spread the giggles, far and near!

## **Threads of Destiny**

In a patchwork quilt of greens and hues,
Threads of fate bind me and you.
With every stitch, a tale unfolds,
Of silly pranks and tales retold.

The daisies whisper secrets sly,
As they plot to make the bees fly by.
They giggle as they spin their yarn,
Dreaming of a glorious dawn.

A floppy leaf declares, "I'm cool!"
While bragging to the other fools.
But every flower knows the score:
The laugh's on them, we want some more!

So here we weave our destinies,
In colors bright, like summer bees.
Together we'll create a scene,
Of floral antics, bright and keen!

## Beginnings in Bloom

In the garden of giggles, sprouts arise,
With socks on their branches, what a surprise!
They dance in the breeze, with tiny green shoes,
While tickling the daisies with playful snooze.

A ladybug waltzes, donning a hat,
As worms pull their weight, or perhaps they just chat!
The sun shines like butter on popcorn galore,
While butterflies joke, 'Who could ask for more?'

Rainclouds play tricks, with a splash and a dash,
But puddles are pools where the frogs like to splash!
When flowers start laughing, oh what a sight,
Their petals are ticklish and oh-so-bright!

In this merry place, joy ropes us in tight,
With every new sprout, a reason to write.
So come join the fun, let your worries take flight,
For beginnings in bloom are pure delight!

## Delicate Visions

In a world where the daisies wear polka-dot hats,
And the robins sing songs of chubby fat cats,
The clouds toss confetti, it's quite the affair,
With giggles and chuckles dancing in the air.

The tulips play poker, but nobody wins,
While the bumblebees buzz 'round like old chums with spins.
They sip on sweet nectar, such fanciful dreams,
In a playful ballet, they twirl and they gleam.

There's a sunflower's joke that brings down the house,
While its petal-friends snicker, "Oh, quiet, you mouse!"
With laughter as bright as a rainbow's first light,
Delicate visions take off in their flight.

So dance through these meadows, bring smiles to your face,
In a symphony of joy, let's find our own place.
With each silly whisper and whimsical scene,
We'll cherish the moments where we all convene.

## The Garden of Infinite Dreams

In a garden where wishes are planted like seeds,
The carrots wear capes while the cabbage just pleads.
With gophers in tuxedos, they throw fancy balls,
And roses roll giggling, pushing down the walls.

The nightingales croon, but they sing out of tune,
While the moon plays the piano made out of cocoon.
A squirrel writes sonnets to the soft, shining stars,
As veggies take bets on the latest moon cars.

In this land of pure laughter where odd things can bloom,
The daisies hold parties in the garden's quaint room.
With snacks made of sunshine and drinks from the rain,
Every moment is silly, vastly comic and plain!

So dig in the soil of this pretty delight,
Where dreams come to life, making clouds feel just right.
And if you should trip over flowers that gleam,
Just laugh with the critters in this garden of dream!

**Lively Impressions**

In the fields of frolic where colors collide,
The violets wear sneakers, they run with such pride.
The sunflowers are gossiping, heads held up high,
While the bees crack their jokes, reaching up to the sky.

With daisies that dazzle and tease with their flair,
They whisper sweet secrets to the bustling air.
A grasshopper juggles the freshest of dew,
As the laughter of petals swirls in a hue.

The butterflies flit like confetti in flight,
Each splash of their colors brings pure delight.
As tulips and zinnias compete for best cheer,
In the carnival garden, the joy's crystal clear!

So waltz through this field, let your worries be few,
For every fresh bloom hides a joke made for you.
With lively impressions, the laughter continues,
In this whimsical playground where silliness ensues!

**Growth in the Gloom**

In a garden where the weeds invade,
A lonely sprout begins to fade.
With a crow's quip and a squirrel's cheer,
It stretches out, 'I'm still right here!'

Raining awkward, the sun plays chummy,
While the flowers dance, their moves quite clumsy.
A daffodil trips, a tulip stumbles,
Yet in this chaos, their laughter rumbles.

A breeze giggles, rustles leaves in jest,
'Why so serious? Just do your best!'
Each petal blushes in comic embrace,
Nature's comedy, in this silly space.

And so they grow, though roots intertwined,
In the gloom of mischief, joy aligned.
With puns and quirks, they all declare,
Who knew growth could be such a funny affair?

## **Shadows Yielding to Light**

In the corners where shadows creep,
A lazy fern stirs from its sleep.
With a chuckle at the sun's bright grin,
It stretches out, 'Oh, let the fun begin!'

A beetle with swagger, all shiny and bold,
Dares the sunbeam, 'I'll not be controlled!'
As the rays tickle, the creatures sway,
In a jig of joy that brightens the day.

The dark's a joker, trying to jest,
'You think you're tough? Well, I'm just a pest!'
Yet as the light pours in, all aglow,
The shadows giggle and start to grow.

They melt away, like ice in the sun,
Leaving behind the warmth—what fun!
A tune of laughter fills the air,
In this bright world, there's joy to share.

## Whispers of Awakening

From beneath the soil, a voice quite meek,
Squeaked a sprout, 'I'm ready to peak!'
With each soft poke of the sun's warm glow,
It jived and jiggled, putting on quite a show.

A ladybug laughed, 'Oh, what a sight!'
As the petals yawned, stretching day and night.
With sleepy blossoms, the tulips snore,
Dreaming of sunshine, a grand encore.

The daisies debated, 'Should we fold or flare?'
In a garden of chaos, they found their flair.
The wind snickered, a playful tease,
'Awake, my friends, now catch that breeze!'

And as they bloomed, giggles filled the glade,
Each flower knowing it had it made.
In whispered secrets, they'd dance and sway,
Awakening through laughter, come what may.

## Blossoms of Hope

Once in a patch where doubts would sprout,
A seed whispered, 'I'll scrounge this out!'
With a giggle and stretch, it reached for the skies,
Determined to blossom, a sweet surprise!

A bumblebee chuckled, 'Let's up the score!'
As petals unfolded, a vibrant encore.
The daisies cheered, in laughter they rolled,
Wishing for sunshine to break from the cold.

They poked at the clouds, with cheeky delight,
'Hey, fluff above, let's play in the light!'
And as rain followed, they danced in the drops,
Finding joy in moments, no matter the hops.

So here they bloom, in colors that cheer,
With shades of the silly, bringing good near.
In the garden of hope, smiles pop and flare,
Each petal a promise, brightening the air.

## The Light Behind the Green

In a garden where the sun does smile,
The plants conspire, just for a while.
One blooms a hat, another a shoe,
They throw a party, just for the view.

The vegetables dance with a vibrant hue,
While sneaky snails play peekaboo.
A radish tells jokes that make you snort,
And carrots form lines for the funniest sort.

The flowers gossip, their petals all fanned,
'Have you seen how tall that weed has planned?'
A sunflower winks, with a cheery grin,
As bumblebees buzz, urging fun to begin.

Amidst the green, laughter does flow,
With photosynthesis putting on a show.
Life in the garden is never a bore,
With every leaf tuning up for encore.

# Awakenings in Quiet Corners

In the dusty nook where the sock monster lurks,
A cabbage reveals all its quirky quirks.
With a wink and a nod, it croons to the floor,
'Who knew I could dance? Come join for some more!'

A potato rolls over, it's quite the sight,
Declaring it's ready to party all night.
The broom joins the jig, sweeps up the dust,
As mice take a break from their usual rust.

Lurking behind books with stories untold,
The herbs play a game of musical gold.
With parsley and thyme setting the tone,
They spin and they twirl, never alone.

When sunlight peeks in through the old window,
The motley crew flourishes, putting on a show.
In quiet corners, there's joy to be found,
With laughter and antics abound all around.

## Gentle Sparks of Awakening

In the dawn where the raindrops drip,
A funny little sprout takes a quick little trip.
'I'm seeking sunshine, it's my favorite treat,'
It hops on the ground, with delight in its feet.

Mushrooms in circles, they start a parade,
'We're the fungi dancers, don't be afraid!'
They wiggle and giggle without a care,
Spreading joy and spores in the morning air.

The daisies unite, their petals aflame,
'Guess what, we've all got the same silly name!'
A bumblebee chuckles, buzzing about,
'You wonderful flowers, it's me you all shout!'

And as twilight creeps with a bow so grand,
The garden holds secrets that tickle the land.
With each gentle spark, a story unfurls,
In the laughter of nature, the magic swirls.

## Flourishing in the Shadows

In the shadows where the odd things grow,
A beetroot cackles, putting on a show.
'Why did the carrot cross the street?'
'To get to the other side for a treat!'

The garlic and onion can't help but laugh,
As they reminisce on their own silly path.
A creeping vine whispers, 'Let's play hide and seek!'
While a sly little chive tries to sneak a peek.

Peeking out behind the old garden bench,
A quirky zucchini makes a funny clench.
'I wear my sweater all day, you see?'
And all of the veggies break out in glee.

In the realm of shadows, there's fun to find,
With whispers and giggles, and silly designs.
So next time you roam where the wild things play,
Join in the laughter, don't shy away!

## Colorful Echoes of Springtime

In gardens where the daisies play,
The bees wear tiny hats all day.
A butterfly, with great delight,
Joins in a jig, what a sight!

The tulips gossip, bright and loud,
Competing hard to draw a crowd.
Ivy climbs, all dressed in green,
Waving at flowers, looking mean!

A rabbit hops, he thinks he's spry,
Chasing shadows, oh my, oh my!
While squirrels plot their daring schemes,
In this garden of silly dreams!

With colors dancing left and right,
Each bloom is ready for a fight.
But laughter twirls in the warm glow,
Springtime's stage, put on a show!

## The Dance of Emerging Life

Tiny sprouts begin to tease,
Swinging gently in the breeze.
Worms with hats strut down the rows,
Showing off their wiggly shows!

Chirping birds join in the fray,
With chirps that brighten up the day.
A frog leaps high, tries to sing,
But croaks come out—oh, what a king!

Blades of grass, they start to sway,
Competing hard to steal the play.
The sun just giggles, shines on bright,
As plants perform with all their might!

Each day a scene, a novel twist,
Nature's tales we can't resist.
In this party full of life,
Humor dances, free from strife!

## Harmonies of Untapped Talent

In the soil, a secret wakes,
Like a joke, it gently shakes.
Roots whisper tunes we can't yet hear,
Filling the garden with cheerful cheer!

Seeds are dreaming underground,
Plotting antics, laughter found.
With every tap and eager push,
The earth is jostled—what a rush!

The cantankerous stones join in,
Rolling around with little grin.
And every sprout that pokes its head,
Eagerly sings, "We aren't dead!"

So let the world hear this refrain,
Life's a party, not in vain.
With nature's humor on display,
There's always fun along the way!

## Nature's Quiet Revelations

The trees wear leaves like fancy hats,
Whispering secrets to the cats.
A breeze slips through, so soft and mild,
As nature giggles, like a child.

The flowers wink, their petals flare,
Creating pranks beyond compare.
A lazy snail moves at a pace,
Believing it's won the great race!

In the shadow, mischief strands,
As ants march off with tiny cans.
Every cricket tunes a song,
While fireflies show where they belong.

Nature's verse, a funny way,
To reveal delights in play.
So here's the truth, as bright as light,
Life is funny—what a sight!

## Enchanted Blooms

In a garden with flowers so bright,
A squirrel tried to take flight.
He tripped on a petal quite large,
Blamed the wind, and then took charge.

Bees were buzzing, doing the dance,
A ladybug thought she'd take a chance.
She slipped on a leaf, oh dear, oh no!
And landed in soil with a humorous 'Whoa!'

The daisies giggled, swayed with the breeze,
As a snail raced by with utmost ease.
But the faster he went, what a funny scene,
He zoomed past the flowers, all green and mean.

Sunflowers chuckled, turning their heads,
As a caterpillar dreamed in his cozy beds.
He opened his eyes, took a peek around,
And lost his cool, tumbled down to the ground.

## Glinting Dreams

In a field where daytime gleams,
Ducks quacked loudly about their dreams.
One wished to sail on a rainbow bright,
While another just chased its tail with delight.

A butterfly, in shades of tinsel,
Landed near, wondering what to wriggle.
She tripped on a blade, fell flat with a thud,
Got up, laughed out loud, and said, 'What a dud!'

Clouds formed tunnels, silly and wide,
A rabbit jumped in and took a ride.
He wobbled and teetered, the clouds shook too,
As laughter erupted like morning dew.

Then a fox, thinking he was a star,
Waltzed with a dream where the wild things are.
He slipped on a twig, gave a twirl and shout,
'Who knew the sky was so close to the ground!'

# The Symphony of Life

In a forest where the critters play,
A frog croaked loud to lead the way.
Birds were chirping in a silly tune,
While a raccoon danced, swaying by the moon.

Squirrels chattered, making quite a fuss,
Chasing their tails on an old, rickety bus.
A turtle watched, moving at his pace,
Said, 'Life's a race? I'm winning, just face it!'

Mice joined in with tiny little feet,
Creating rhythms, oh, what a feat!
A badger drummed on a hollow log,
All joined in for a jam session, oh my dog!

With laughter echoing through the trees,
They spun in circles, danced with ease.
A tune of joy, of love, of cheer,
In this symphony, all was clear.

**Fleeting Moments of Brilliance**

A jester pot in a garden stout,
Telled funny tales, made everyone shout.
A bird flew by with a silly twist,
And promptly sat down on a gleaming list.

Rabbits in hats flipped coins like pros,
While a hedgehog tried to impress with his pose.
But he tripped on his spikes, rolled into a heap,
And laughed, 'Now that's one for the keep!'

Daffodils danced in a bright accord,
Their laughter echoed, even the Lord.
As the sun dipped low, they spun in delight,
Creating brilliant moments, a charming sight.

And as twilight fell, under stars so bright,
The critters gathered for one last bite.
With tales of the day, they giggled and cheered,
Fleeting moments like jewels, perfectly seared.

## A Palette of Promise

Colors spill from every jar,
Paintbrushes dance like a guitar.
Splashes of red, a twirl of blue,
Who knew art could stick like glue?

Canvases await with eager charm,
Yet sometimes, they might bring alarm.
A sneeze with paint? Oh, what a sight!
Monet could never, try as he might!

Mixing hues gets a bit wild,
Like toddlers with cake—all reviled!
Every swirl tells a silly tale,
As laughter fills the colorful trail.

So here's to the joy, the giggles so sweet,
Where even a canvas can dance to the beat.
With brushes in hand and mischief in air,
Art with a grin is beyond compare!

**Traces of Brilliance**

In the garden, chaos reigns supreme,
Flowers giggle, it's quite the dream.
With petals strewn on the ground so loud,
A blooming mess, and we're all so proud!

Bees buzz around like they own the place,
With pollen on their heads, oh what a race!
Chasing butterflies in a dizzying swirl,
Nature laughs, giving chaos a twirl.

Worms wriggle like they're in a dance,
While squirrels chat, sharing a glance.
"Who's the prettiest?" they chirp and tease,
As the daffodils bloom in a bright yellow breeze!

Each blossom tells jokes that petals impart,
A bouquet of laughter, a work of art.
So in this tangle of nature's delight,
Find giggles and joy, from morning to night!

## The Elegance of Emerge

Out from the soil, a sprout appears,
With tiny leaves and lots of cheers.
Wobbling young in the morning sun,
A plant's first dance, oh boy, what fun!

Tripping over roots, it starts to climb,
A silly stumble—who needs a rhyme?
Each leaf a giggle, each stem a jest,
Nature's prankster on a whim to invest.

The clouds above begin to rain,
"Grow up!" they shout, "Stop acting insane!"
While flowers bloom with a wink and a nod,
Emerging like stars from the quirkiest pod.

So here's to the growth, a raucous affair,
With roots in the ground and dreams in the air.
Nature's tease, through the sunshine she glows,
The elegance of growth, as laughter bestows!

**Fluttering Hues**

Birds paint the air with feathers bright,
Flapping their wings, they take flight.
A splash of color, from yellow to red,
In this artful sky, joy is widespread!

Butterflies giggle as they flit and fly,
With every twist, they wink at the sky.
"Try to catch us!" they flutter and tease,
As they sip sweet nectar, a moment of ease.

The breeze joins in with a cheeky grin,
Whispering secrets where the fun begins.
Nature's palette, in shades so grand,
Who knew flying could be so unplanned?

So let's dance with colors, let laughter ensue,
As the world is awash in a whimsical hue.
With each flutter, we'll chase the light,
Where hues double-take in pure delight!

## **Rays of Potential**

In a garden of thoughts, seeds do sprout,
Chasing sunshine while giggling out loud.
Each little thought, like a curious flea,
Jumping around, oh, so carefree!

With watering cans and wild imagination,
They dance in the breeze, full of elation.
Sprouts of ideas, some quirky, some bright,
Shining like stars in the giggly night.

A worm told a joke, and the daisies turned red,
While the carrots just laughed, 'Look, we're well-fed!'
Branches all shaking, a comedic display,
It's a riot out here, what more can I say?

So here's to the seedlings, the dreams on the rise,
Winking and sharing their all-time best ties.
Together they form a jubilant throng,
Spreading the cheer, where everything's strong!

**The Journey to Luminosity**

One day a seed said, 'I want to be great!'
But first it must wiggle, not hurry, or wait.
On the path to the light, it tripped on a bug,
And tumbled right down with a giggly shrug.

With sunlight ahead, it turned to a friend,
'Let's race to the limit, it's fun to pretend!'
But the turtle replied, 'Slow down, little pal,
Life isn't a sprint; it's a comedy gal!'

Through puddles and laughter, they ventured anew,
With a wink and a chuckle, what fun they would brew!
The journey brought joy, not just to find fame,
But jumping through puddles, the best kind of game!

So nurture the dreams that make little hearts sing,
For laughter is magic, a wonderful thing.
When chased by the sun, there's no need to rush,
Just take little steps, and enjoy the big hush!

## Spheres of Ecstasy

In the garden of wonder, the blooms had a bash,
With petals like party hats, vibrant and brash.
They spun in circles, embracing the breeze,
With a wink and a giggle, as light as the tease.

Each blossom erupted in fits of delight,
Floating like bubbles, they danced into night.
"Who knew we could giggle?" a daffodil said,
While chuckling and bouncing, they bounced on ahead!

The sun gave a chuckle as it peeked through the trees,
"Keep up the fun, friends, be as silly as bees!"
With laughter like raindrops, they twirled with such glee,
In a whirl of colors, oh, what a spree!

So treasure the joy that each moment can bring,
Even petals of laughter can shine like a king.
In the spheres of pure joy, let your spirit take flight,
For the garden's a stage, and we're one wild delight!

## Eclipsed Light

In shadows they gathered, the sprightly young crew,
Preparing a party, oh, if they only knew!
With flashlights for beams and a blanket for shade,
They thought they'd eclipse the sun, how they played!

Around came a beetle, with wise little eyes,
"Who can eclipse sunshine? You're in for surprise!"
They giggled and spun, with a twirl and a whir,
"Let's dance with the shadows, let laughter concur!"

A moth made a toast, in the name of the night,
"Unite, dear friends, in our giggly delight!"
With chuckles and cheer, they stole the dark stage,
For shadows are silly, and laughter, the sage!

So here's to the moments when light meets a grin,
When eclipsing the worries lets the fun begin.
With friendship and laughter, the stars shine so bright,
Together we'll shine, even in the dim light!

## Sparkling Visions in the Soil

In the dirt, where dreams do sprout,
Worms twist with glee, there's no doubt.
They wiggle and squirm, plump and round,
Craving sunlight, they dance on the ground.

With each little seed, the mischief grows,
A tomato thinks it can wear a nose.
Peas play tag with some radish friends,
In this garden madness, laughter never ends.

Bees buzz along like they own the place,
Mocking the flowers who can't keep pace.
A sunflower's tall with a silly grin,
"Bet you can't reach me!" it shouts with a spin.

So dig in the dirt and find your cheer,
In this garden realm, silliness is here!
Join the plant party, wear a leaf hat,
You'll find joy growing, just like that!

## Petals in the Golden Hour

Golden light spills like lemonade,
While grasshoppers dance, unafraid.
Daisies stare at the sun with delight,
"Is it just me, or is this quite a sight?"

A dandy lion dons a fluffy crown,
"Look at me! I'm the king of this town!"
With every gust, they wave and sway,
Telling each other, "Let's seize the day!"

Butterflies join in a wobbly flight,
Trying to look cool, but losing their sight.
"Oops! Did I land on a dog's shiny nose?"
"Oops! You're the fanciest flower, I suppose!"

As twilight descends, the fun doesn't stop,
Fireflies flicker like confetti on top.
The night blooms with giggles, pure and clear,
In this garden of whimsy, soon will appear!

## Glimmers of Hope in Every Sprout

Each little sprout has a tale to tell,
From the muck of the earth, they're doing well.
With leaves that giggle under the sun,
"Did you see me tower? Oh, wasn't that fun?"

A mushroom pops up with such flair,
"Just your average fungi, beyond compare!"
They twirl and they twist, a bouncy surprise,
Poking fun at the clouds, trading wisecrack replies.

Caterpillars munch with a rhythmic chew,
"Are we almost done? I got stuff to do!"
While bees buzz around, silly in flight,
"Let's pollinate flowers, hey, this feels right!"

As sunshine showers and laughter grows,
Around each green sprout, a giggle blooms,
So dance, little plants, to nature's sweet song,
In this wacky world, together we belong!

## Awakening the Hidden Splendor

In the gloom, a bloom starts to snack,
On nutrients hidden, not looking back.
It wiggles and jiggles, all tucked in tight,
"Time to pop out and shine, alright!"

Worms hold a meeting beneath the ground,
"Did you hear? A flower's getting unbound!"
They clink soil cups, their laughter a cheer,
"Go, little sprout! Show the world here!"

Sunbeams spill in like glittery cake,
Painting the garden for goodness' sake.
A cactus chuckles, "I'm green but cute,
Prickly on edges, but oh, what a hoot!"

So let them all blossom, it's time for a spree,
In a world where the wild plants roam free.
With jests and with jives, life ticks like a clock,
Nature's kooky venture—welcome to the flock!

**Flourish and Soar**

Tiny seeds in the ground,
Dreaming of skies unbound.
With a sprinkle of cheer,
They'll soon burst out here!

Wiggly leaves in a dance,
Nature's own funny prance.
Their giggles tickle the air,
As they twirl without a care.

Bouncing blossoms take flight,
In a prankster's delight.
Watch them leap, twist, and shout,
Who knew plants could be stout?

So let your spirit grow,
Join in this wild show.
Laugh with petals that soar,
Watch them all beg for more!

## Ethereal Flare

In the garden, a spark,
A flower begins to embark.
With a hiccup and a wink,
It's the bright pink's time to drink!

A daffodil cracks a joke,
To a shocked weary oak.
But the tree, in its deep voice,
Said, "You think I had a choice?"

Glowing colors take the stage,
As if flipping a new page.
Behind the petals, a grin,
A carnival under the skin!

With every colorful cheer,
Laughter spreads wide and near.
In this wacky sunny flair,
All join in the zany air!

## **A Tapestry of Radiance**

Threads of green weave a tale,
Of joyous weeds that prevail.
They conspire in a plot,
To make us giggle a lot!

Look at the rose with a smirk,
Like a kid pulling a quirk.
It whispers sweet little lies,
While the daisies roll their eyes!

As sunlight drips through the leaves,
The smiley flowers achieve.
With respect, they interlace,
Bright chaos in this place!

Each petal wears a funny hat,
Daring the world, "Can you top that?"
In this loud, colorful scene,
Nature's jesters reign supreme!

## **Shards of Illumination**

Glowing gems on stalks so tall,
They dance and twirl without a fall.
With a wink and a silly cheer,
They draw in every passerby near.

Petals laugh, bumblebees buzz,
What a ruckus, oh what a fuzz!
Who knew blossoms could be clowns?
Playing games in flowery gowns!

Through the garden, joy does race,
With a daisy in a playful chase.
"Catch me if you can!" it sings,
As laughter fills the air with wings!

At twilight, colors collide,
Even the stars can't hide their pride.
In this splendid riot of light,
Every bloom's a sheer delight!

## When Petals Speak

In gardens where the daisies giggle,
And roses wear their shiny wiggle,
The petals whisper jokes at noon,
While bees dance like a clumsy cartoon.

With every bloom, a sly remark,
They gossip 'neath the old oak park,
"Why did the flower cross the street?"
To show off its style and its beat!

Tulips tell tales of windy days,
Where breezes played in funny ways,
While violets snicker, losing grace,
With pollen sneezes all over the place.

So if you wander through this scene,
Remember flowers love to glean,
A laugh, a cheer, a bright display,
In nature's wacky, wild ballet.

## The Awakening Palette

In fields of green, the colors jive,
Awake, alive, where hues arrive,
The red blooms tease the yellow sun,
"Bet you can't catch me, I'm too fun!"

With each petal, a splash of cheer,
The purple waves all draw you near,
Chasing shades with silly tricks,
Dancing here, the hopscotch mix.

The daisies leap in polka dots,
While sunflowers call out funny shots,
"Why so serious?" they all sing,
As grasshoppers join in a spring fling!

So grab a brush, let laughter soar,
In this garden of hues, explore,
Where colors play and giggles grow,
In a wild, whimsical, kaleidoscope show.

## A Symphony in Bloom

The flowers join for a grand parade,
In bloom attire, a laughter cascade,
"Let's start with a waltz!" the poppies say,
As the pansies join in a funny sway.

The daisies strike up a bright girly tune,
While lilacs nod under the laughing moon,
A sunflower plays the trumpet loud,
As the peonies tease the sleepy crowd.

The tulips clap with their feathery hands,
Mimicking beats like silly bands,
"Let's take it higher!" they shout with glee,
As the wind plays the world's best symphony.

In this concert of nature's delight,
Where blooms and laughter ignite the night,
Join the revel, let your worries flee,
In a whimsical twist of harmonies.

## Colors Unfurling

Oh, look at that daffodil's prank,
With petals like sails on a cheerful bank,
"Catch me if you can!" it shouts so bold,
While marigolds giggle, their secrets untold.

The crocuses cheer from the snowy white
Beneath the sun's watch, they feel so bright,
"Why are flowers always bright and merry?"
"Because they bloom when life gets cherry!"

Carnations dance in their polka dot shoes,
While lilacs wear gowns in vibrant hues,
They twirl and spin, feeling quite grand,
With petals that wave like a jolly hand.

So saunter through the hues that play,
In a garden where colors laugh and sway,
With every bloom, a funny refrain,
A tapestry rich with cheer and no pain.

## Dawn of Possibilities

In the early light, we giggle and sway,
The sun's peeking out, what a silly display!
Flowers in pajamas, stretching their heads,
Bouncing with laughter, as daybreak spreads.

Little ants marching, a parade on the ground,
All wearing tiny hats, oh what a sound!
They dance with their crumbs, a feast on the floor,
Morning's just starting, who could ask for more?

Bright morning dew, a laugh in its shine,
Like jewels on the grass, they sparkle and twine.
Birds cracking jokes from branches up high,
It's nature's own sitcom, oh me, oh my!

With each silly petal, they wink and they moon,
Whispering secrets, beneath the bright moon.
Life's quirky canvas, vivid and grand,
Painting our mornings, a comical brand.

# **Glimmers of Joy**

A tadpole hops by, with bubbles of glee,
Carrying secrets, as happy as can be.
Each wiggle, each splash, a dance in the stream,
Oh, what a sight! We all start to beam.

Dandelions laughing, tossed by the breeze,
Making wishes on spores, floating with ease.
They know all the tricks, how to giggle and play,
Transforming dull patches into bright ballet.

Bees buzzing tunes, high notes on their flight,
Crafting sweet symphonies, from morn until night.
Collecting the nectar, a sugary ride,
In a hive full of giggles, they all take pride.

With every warm sunlight, we share playful grins,
In nature's own game, everyone wins!
A riot of colors, where laughter is crowned,
In a world that's alive, joy's waiting around.

## **Radiant Journeys**

A snail with a backpack, on a grand little quest,
Taking the slow route, but he likes it best!
With tattered maps made of leaves, oh so neat,
He waves to the pebbles, his munching is sweet.

Butterflies zipping, like confetti in flight,
Right past the snail who shouts, "What a sight!"
They giggle and twirl, as they flutter and glide,
While snail takes his time on this colorful ride.

Toadstools act classy, in their polka dot wear,
Sipping on raindrops, without a single care.
In a world full of fluff and a sprinkle of cheer,
Every creature is part of this wonderful sphere.

As sunshine spills laughter over hilltops so bright,
Nature's a circus, with wonders in sight.
Each journey we take, full of whimsy and song,
In the laughter of life, we all belong.

**The Color of Growth**

With crayons of sunshine, the grass starts to sing,
A symphony painted, on the back of a spring.
Seeds in their beds, telling stories so wild,
Of dreams that are sprouting, and secrets compiled.

The caterpillar frumps, then suddenly leaps,
Turns into a bright flier, oh how nature keeps!
With wings like a canvas, of colors galore,
Joking with flowers, "Who's the brightest of four?"

Comical mushrooms, with hats on their heads,
Throwing a party in the patches and spreads.
Inviting the raindrops to join in the fun,
With laughter that echoes beneath the warm sun.

In the theater of growth, where whispers unite,
Funky little plants compete for the light.
Each day a new canvas, with joy as our taupe,
Here's to the silly and boundless, our hope!

## Whispers of Hidden Potential

In a garden where dreams grow wide,
The veggies joke, they never hide.
Carrots wear glasses, oh what a sight,
As radishes giggle with sheer delight.

Tomatoes roll on the ground with glee,
While peppers dance, oh so carefree.
Each seed's a comedian, waiting to sprout,
With punchlines ready, there's never a drought.

The lettuce is laughing, it's quite a tease,
Hiding behind onions, they wiggle with ease.
A silly cucumber joins the fun,
In this garden, everyone's number one!

So remember this garden when you feel blue,
There's laughter in growth, just waiting for you.
With comedic roots and leafy dreams,
Every sprout's a star, or so it seems!

## **Seeds of Radiant Hopes**

In the soil where giggles take flight,
Tiny seeds plan a comedy night.
The sunflower claims the role of the host,
While daisies laugh, they'll be great at most!

The beans tell jokes about climbing too high,
While peas make puns with a twinkle in eye.
Each sprout has a tale, full of charm,
With humor in growth, it's never a harm.

The pumpkins joke about Halloween fame,
They dress up in costumes, all in the game!
As broccoli tries to become a stand-up star,
His punchlines are veggies, so strange yet bizarre.

So let your garden be a place to laugh,
With plants and their jokes on a silly half.
In the earth where bright hopes will rise,
You'll find happiness hidden in every surprise!

**Blossoms in the Morning Mist**

As morning dew kisses petals so bright,
A sunflower yawns, what a silly sight!
Rosebuds chuckle, they're just waking up,
While lilies sip tea from a tiny cup.

The mist giggles softly, it joins the fun,
With butterflies dancing, the show's just begun.
Every blossom a player, in nature's grand play,
With humor and laughter to start off the day!

Mornings in gardens are never bland,
With tulips cracking jokes, more fun than planned.
The peonies whisper the best of the day,
While honeysuckles hum a sweet ballet.

So ride the breeze of delightful cheer,
Where flowers bloom with joy, never fear.
In the morning mist, all jokes take flight,
Nature's own comedy, a true delight!

## **Petals of Promise Unfurled**

With petals poised and tales to unfold,
Roses dictate stories, brimming with bold.
Violets chuckle, they can't keep still,
Their wit is sharp, blooming at will.

In the flowerbed, secrets they share,
Planters plot mischief without a care.
A zinnia winks, 'Are you ready to laugh?'
While marigolds giggle, 'We're on the right path!'

The geraniums dance in delight all around,
As daisies spin tales that wear a crown.
With petals so vibrant, and smiles so bright,
A garden comedy that's bound to excite!

So come and enjoy this festival of cheer,
Where every bloom brings giggles near.
With whispers of humor in every swirl,
Nature's vignette of promise unfurl!

## Hidden Treasures

Underneath the old oak tree,
Lies a treasure, not a key.
Beneath the dirt, a sock I found,
Smells like cheese, best left unbound.

In my pocket, a fuzzy worm,
Claims it leads to riches firm.
But all it gives is endless laughs,
And sticky, gooey science crafts.

A rusty coin, a crumpled snack,
I keep them close; they're never slack.
A world of oddities we hide,
Like lost socks' secret, filled with pride!

What lies beneath the surface brown,
Are giggles from the underground.
For every laugh that's surely fled,
A treasure's waiting, laugh instead!

## A Canvas of Colors

A paintbrush dipped in jelly beans,
Swirls of laughter, candy scenes.
Brush the sky in polka dots,
And make the grass with glitter spots.

Dandelions in bright neon hues,
Tickling toes in candy shoes.
With every splash of silly paint,
The flowers giggle, faint but quaint.

My cat dons a paint-splattered hat,
Waltzing round with a colorful bat.
Each small stroke brings gleeful sound,
And colors dance upon the ground.

In this madcap, vivid spree,
Art is fun, just wait and see!
Throw your worries in a bowl,
And serve them fresh with laughter's roll!

## **Seeds of Change**

Plant a seed, a silly one,
Water it with lemonade fun.
Watch it grow with giggles wide,
A dancing plant—our goofy guide.

In the garden, socks take flight,
As worms wear hats and dance at night.
Sprouting laughter, row by row,
The weirdest flowers start to glow.

Chickens cluck in polka dot,
Bodies shaking, strutting hot!
What a change in every glance,
Nature's weird and wild dance.

When life gives seeds, plant with cheer,
And watch the silliness appear.
For change is good, and fun's the game,
With every sprout, it's never tame!

## In the Garden of Thought

In the garden of what we think,
Grows a tree of bubble drink.
Branches bend with juicy puns,
Fruits of laughter, just for fun!

A patch of worries blooms with fear,
Snip them off, make giggles clear.
We tend the thoughts like little sprouts,
Whispers of joy in all the shouts.

Scarecrows made of odd ideas,
Dance around and spread their cheers.
Every critter has a quirk,
In this place, they go berserk!

So wander through this mindy grove,
Where silly tales and giggles rove.
With every step, a chuckle springs,
In the garden where laughter sings!

www.ingramcontent.com/pod-product-compliance
Lightning Source LLC
Chambersburg PA
CBHW071831160426
43209CB00003B/276